Compound Scroll Saw Creations

By Diana Thompson

Fox
Chapel Publishing Co. Inc.

1970 Broad Street • East Petersburg, PA 17520 • www.foxchapelpublishing.com

Compound Scroll Saw Creations is a brand new work, first published in 2002 by Fox Chapel Publishing Company, Inc. The patterns contained herein are copyrighted by the author. Artists purchasing this book have permission to make up to 200 cutouts of each individual pattern. Persons or companies wishing to make more than 200 cutouts must request permission from the author in writing. The patterns themselves, however, are not to be duplicated for resale or distribution under any circumstances.

Publisher	Alan Giagnocavo
Project Editor	Ayleen Stellhorn
Desktop Specialist	Linda L. Eberly, Eberly Designs Inc.
Cover Design	Keren Holl

ISBN # 1–56523–170–8

To order your copy of this book,
please send check or money order
for the cover price plus $3.50 shipping to:
Fox Books
1970 Broad Street
East Petersburg, PA 17520

Or visit us on the web at
www.foxchapelpublishing.com

Printed in China
10 9 8 7 6 5 4 3 2

Because scrolling wood and other materials inherently includes the risk of injury and damage, this book cannot guarantee that creating the projects in this book is safe for everyone. For this reason, this book is sold without warranties or guarantees of any kind, express or implied, and the publisher and author disclaim any liability for any injuries, losses or damages caused in any way by the content of this book or the reader's use of the tools needed to complete the projects presented here. The publisher and the author urge all scrollers to thoroughly review each project and to understand the use of all tools involved before beginning any project.

Acknowledgments
Thank you Father for the over abundance of blessing.
Thank you Bill and Connie for your time, effort, and encouragement.
Most of all, thank you for your love!

Table of Contents

Introduction

"Caution: Compound Sawing is addictive"

Two years ago I discovered a tiny little 3-D pattern on a web site. Of course I had to try it! Since that time, I've been totally addicted to compound sawing. The adventure has been one of the greatest experiences of my life and one I plan to continue for a long time to come. Not only have I discovered a new career, but I have met the world's kindest people—scroll sawers like yourself, and the talented people at Fox Chapel Publishing who do such a wonderful job of presenting my work.

It's my goal to make compound sawing as enjoyable for others as it is for me. Over the past year I've learned many new things, thanks to experimenting and helpful tips from other scrollers. I've passed along what I've found that works for me and hope that it will for you, too. And as always, I welcome any suggestions.

Once again, the inspiration has come from so many different areas.

My golfing buddy, Barb, designs tee shirts for different occasions and gave me permission to make a figure of her caterpillar design.

The "Apple for the Teacher" was adapted from a pattern in my first book. Having heard that first pattern called "Apple for the Teacher," I was reminded of a teacher whom I didn't particularly like—hence the worm!

The Cactus came into being when another golfing buddy, Sharon, asked me for a Christmas ornament with a southwest flavor. The cactus pattern looked rather plain, so I added a rattlesnake using it as a lookout. (Can rattle snakes climb??? If they can't, don't tell me!)

While on a snorkeling trip to Destin, Florida, a blue heron posed long enough for me to get a good sketch of him. He stood still so long, I began to think he was rather vain and proud of himself.

Miss Martha was inspired by Martha Stewart. I happened to see her on television one day around Easter time making cotton ball bunnies. The instant I saw that I knew the bunny would make a great compound pattern.

It's my great pleasure to present these new designs in the hopes that you will enjoy making them as much as I enjoy bringing them to life.

With best regards,
Diana Thompson
scrollergirl@aol.com
www.scrollsawinspirations.com

CHAPTER ONE

About Compound Sawing

Compound sawing is simply making two cuts on the same working stock to achieve a three-dimensional figure. The pattern consists of two sides: the front and profile views. The left side is cut first; then the right side. For such a simple concept, it turns out some fantastic figures, which look much more complicated than they are. You will mystify all those who are not familiar with the concept. Others have told me the figures are impossible to do on a scroll saw. I just laugh and keep right on designing and cutting.

Trouble Shooting

The following tips are things I have found helpful when cutting the figures. You're welcome to use them and pass along any new ones you discover.

The Blades

All my patterns call for using a #5 single or skip tooth milled blade. There are several good brands on the market, so experiment and choose the one that works best for you. I prefer the single tooth, but that's a matter of preference on my part. Change your blade often. A dull blade will make cutting very slow and difficult.

Tension the blade properly. If you find it's taking a lot of pressure to cut the wood or your blade is moving around like a worm, it very well could be that the tension is not tight enough.

I don't recommend using a reverse tooth blade. It tends to slow down the saw action. A reverse tooth blade can also be a little more difficult to control.

Beginning scrollers should keep in mind that a milled blade will track off to the right due to the manufacturing process. Sometimes it helps to run a diamond hone along the back edge of the blade while the saw is running. This will remove the edge that causes the blade to track. Having said that, it really isn't all that difficult to control the blade once you're aware that it will track. Simply cock your work a little to the left.

There is another type of scroll saw blade on the market called "precision ground." This blade is ground instead of milled, which does solve the tracking problem of a milled blade. They are very aggressive and sharp, which is good; but if you make a mistake, it's usually fatal to your project and you may have to start over again. Precision ground blades are also expensive.

With compound sawing, it's important that your blade is properly aligned straight up and down. Just making sure your table is level does not ensure that the blade is aligned. Remove the table insert and lay a small metal ruler up against the blade. Move the saw arm up and down, gently, by hand. The blade should move up and down beside the ruler without moving the ruler left or right. Consult the owner's manual of your particular saw if you need to make a blade adjustment.

When cutting the thicker, 1 1/2" stock, it's sometimes difficult to keep the feed running straight into the blade, especially when making sharp turns. Beginners tend to push the blade sideways, instead of allowing it to run truly straight up and down. A conscious effort is needed to solve this problem. You will feel the saw bog down a little after making a turn, like it's becoming harder to cut. The work may also jump up and down. Back off just a little, let the blade right itself, then continue sawing. You will soon be aware of what is happening and will automatically back off.

The Saw Table

To ensure a smooth, level surface, I have cut a piece of Plexiglas to the size of my saw table and cut a 1/4" hole in the center for the blade opening. Not all table inserts are level with the table, which will cause distorted figures when they fall into this uneven surface. Also, smaller figures may fall through the insert opening, never to be found again. Two pieces of two-sided 3/4" tape hold it on easily.

With use, the Plexiglas will roughen up. When that happens just polish it with a paste wax as you would the saw table. Between polishing, give it a few buffs now and then with a shop cloth or old tee shirt material. While cutting the Plexiglas to fit your table, leave the plastic film on or apply masking tape to keep the Plexiglas from melting back onto itself as you cut. Slow the feed down to about 1100 strokes per minute and use a #7 or larger blade.

Clear Packing Tape

Because one side of the patterns call for using 1 1/2" stock, which is pretty thick for the scroll saw, I've found that covering all my wood with clear packing tape makes it easier to saw. At first I only used the

tape on the harder woods, such as black walnut, to keep the wood from burning. I have since found that the application of tape makes all types of wood easier and faster to cut. No one knows for sure why this works, but the popular theory is the adhesive in the tape lubricates the blade. The glare on the tape from work lights can make it difficult to see, so apply the tape first, then the pattern on top. I guarantee this tip will make your sawing much more enjoyable.

Spray Adhesive

Spray adhesive is the best way to apply the patterns to the working stock. Give the patterns a good, healthy spray. The remaining paper won't have to be removed as with most scroll sawing. If you have trouble getting the pattern straight on the wood, give it an extra good spray and slide the pattern around until it's in the proper position.

Like spray paint, the adhesive will go all over the place, so a spray box comes in handy. Simply place a grate, tilted at a 45-degree angle, inside a cardboard box and spray away. I use a piece of cut-off shelving in mine. Poultry netting (aka chicken wire) works well too.

Helpful Tools

The tools on this list may make your work go faster, but they are not necessary.

• Rotary tool inserted in a drill press attachment:

A Plexiglas cover over the saw table will make objects move much smoother across the surface.

A spray box will keep spray glue from spreading all over your shop.

This tool comes in handy for drilling starter holes.

• Rotary tool inserted in a router table: Use this tool to round over the edges of the carousel platform.

• Stationary sander: A stationary sander comes in handy for squaring the ends of working stock and the bottom of many of the patterns. Also, it can be used to sand the angles of the carousel box and roof.

• Drill press: Placing your project in a vise and using a drill press ensures a perfectly straight drilling task, as when drilling the holes for the horses in the carousel project.

• Forstner bit: This is a special bit made for drilling a perfect hole, which comes in handy for making the clocks and candlestick projects.

   The hand tools listed below (and shown in the photo at the right) are also very useful.

• Small vise for holding your project still while measuring or drilling with the drill press

• Manual drill to drill screw starter holes and/or pilot holes in the patterns

• Assorted drill bits, ranging from 1/16" to 1/4"

• Quick Grips or other small grips

A variety of hand tools (listed at left and below) will aid in making compound scroll saw figures.

• A ruler for measuring and testing the saw blade alignment

• Pony clamps for gluing stock together

• A medium size screwdriver for general purposes

• Small screwdrivers for special purposes

• A square for general measuring and to align the saw blade

• Craft knife for general trimming

Have you ever noticed the hole in the middle of the sanding disk?

There is nothing behind that spot to support the sanding disk and when you're sanding a wider project. As a result, there will be a bump in the middle that doesn't get sanded down. This really interferes when trying to glue parts together. It will cause gaps at each end. There is a way to remedy this. Fill the hole with ordinary modeling clay. When it dries, sand it level and replace the sanding disk. If for any reason the disk itself needs to be removed, the clay can be removed in seconds.

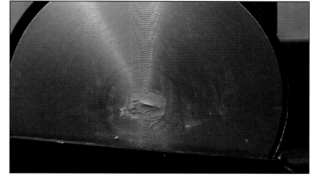

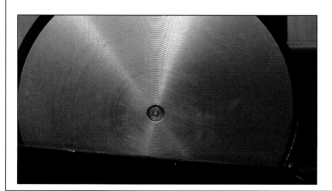

CHAPTER TWO

Wood for Compound Scrolling

I like to use a wide variety of wood for compound scrolling. The photos in this section will give you a good idea of the different characteristics of many woods. I've based the ease or difficulty of cutting each species on working with 1¹/2" stock. Any of these woods will cut easily when using thinner stock. Each sample has been finished with one coat of wood sealer and several coats of high-gloss clear acrylic spray.

Group I (Very Easy)

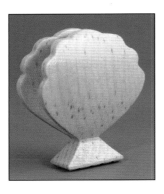

1. Sugar Pine
This is the softest and easiest wood to cut. I use it for all my pattern testing and for the figures I plan to paint. This wood is excellent for beginners just learning to compound saw. A very pleasant wood with which to work.

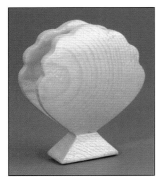

2. White Pine
White pine works nearly as well as sugar pine. It also has the advantage of being readily available at most home improvement stores. Look for lumber free of knots and as clear-white as possible. Sometimes it has hard grains that make it a little difficult to cut.

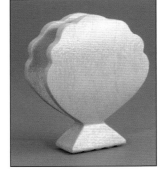

3. Basswood
This wood is easy to saw and is also a good one to use for painted projects because of its light color. It isn't particularly interesting left in its natural state.

4. Redwood
Redwood is easy to cut. It has a rather dull brown color but finishes nicely. It does have a strong aroma when sawn, but a respirator mask takes care of the odor.

5. Aspen
Aspen has a nice white appearance and a satin sheen when finished. The wood is fuzzy when cut and will dull the blade quickly. This is a good wood for painting because the grain is rather nondescript.

Group II (Easy)

1. Lacewood
This wood has an interesting giraffe-like appearance. Due to the hard and soft areas in the grain, the wood will jump around a little when cutting. Extra effort should be taken to hold the work firmly down on the saw table. Finishes nicely.

2. Red Cedar
Red cedar has a very beautiful red color and finishes lovely. It also cuts smoothly. The strong aroma calls for a respirator mask. Another of my favorites.

3. Spanish Cedar
This variety of cedar cuts very easily and finishes nicely. It has a nice golden brown tint, which makes it pleasant in appearance. Very pungent aroma while sawing.

7. Willow
This wood is easy to cut and has very interesting grains and colors. It takes a little extra effort to get a smooth finish, but the difficulty is well worth the effort. Another favorite.

4. Heart of the Cypress
A most beautiful, soft golden color and a creamy, velvety appearance are typical of this wood. The heart of cypress does not have the hard grains found in the sapwood. It is a most delightful wood to work with and another of my favorites.

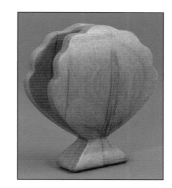

5. Alder
Alder has a nice reddish-brown color. It finishes and cuts fairly easily. Unfortunately, it is not the most interesting of woods as it is usually very uniform in appearance. This sample has a rare appearance.

6. Canary Wood
Canary wood has lots of interesting grains and colors, including pink at times. It is easy to cut and finish. I find this wood a pleasure to cut. It is another of my favorites.

8. Ordinary 3/4" Birch plywood
This wood cuts nicely and has an interesting appearance due to the layers in the product. As with the particle board, glue is used in the manufacturing and will dull the blade quickly.

Group III (Not So Easy)

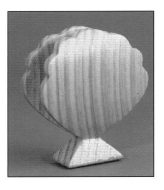

1. Cypress, sapwood
The sapwood of a cypress tree is a little more difficult to cut than the heartwood, but the prominent grains make it interesting to cut. It reminds me of a zebra. Finishes fairly easily.

2. Mahogany
This wood cuts smoothly and finishes to a beautiful dark, rich color.

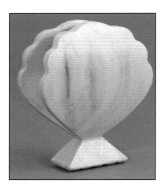

3. Magnolia
Magnolia is a most beautiful wood, especially the heart wood. The sapwood is creamy white, but the heartwood has lovely gray to black to purple streaks that make it very interesting. It has a velvety appearance and finishes fantastically! One of my very favorites.

4. Particle board
I tried this material on a whim. It's an interesting concept, and the appearance is different. The only major drawback is the glue used to make the product. It dulls the saw blade quickly. (Photo)

Group IV (Not Easy At All)

1. Black Walnut
This wood is a woodworkers dream. It cuts smoothly, with little or no sanding, and finishes perfectly. When using it for a bigger figure, you may have to change your blade for the second cut. Be patient and let the saw blade do its work at its own speed. My all-time favorite hardwood.

2. Lauan
Lauan is very dense, but it can be used. This wood cuts much like black walnut and finishes fairly nice. (Photo)

3. Red Oak
I've added this wood because it seems to be a favorite of woodworkers. It cuts similarly to lauan, but it will jump around a bit. Extra effort will be needed to hold the work flat to the saw table. Not my most favorite to use, but it will finish nicely.

4. Corian®
Corian is a solid surface material, manufactured by Du Pont. It is used mainly for kitchen and bathroom counter tops. Slow the saw speed down to about 1100 strokes per minute, and cover the Corian with masking tape before cutting. These steps will keep the material from melting back onto itself. If you don't see material coming from inside the kerf as you cut, the saw speed is probably too fast. There are several saw blades on the market recommended for cutting solid surface material.

CHAPTER THREE

Compound How-to

The following steps will show you the easiest and quickest method to cut compound figures. Some of the patterns will have frets, which are inside cuts. In this case, cut the frets first, starting with the left side of the pattern, then the right side. Smaller frets can be discarded; larger ones should be left in the block to give the figure stability and hold it firmly in place.

Important note: For the best results, cut to the waste side of the lines. Some of the patterns are quite delicate, such as the butterfly, and removing too much material will cause easy breakage.

100%

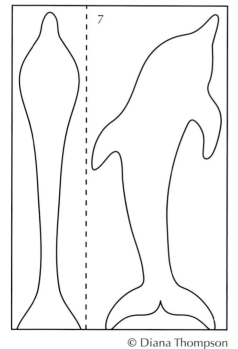

© Diana Thompson

Cutting

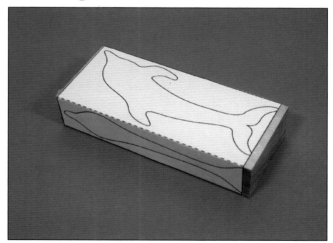

Step 1. Fold pattern along the dashed line, and adhere it to the stock with spray adhesive.

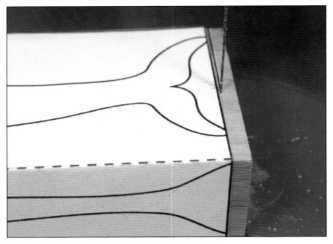

Step 2. Saw across the bottom edge (above) or sand it even with disk sander (below). At this point, make any inside cuts if called for on the pattern.

Step 3. Cut out the left side in one continuous line.

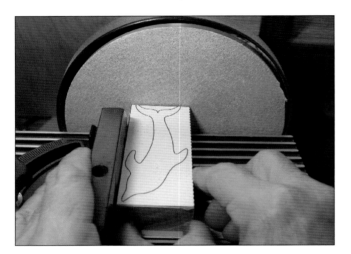

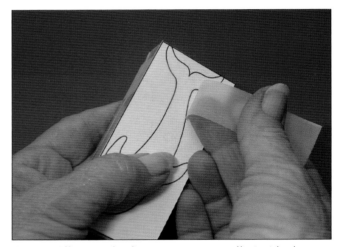

Step 4. Allowing the figure to rest naturally inside the block, pinch the wood together and tape around it in one or two places, depending on the size of your project. This step helps to hold the figure in the block. It also keeps the top portion from tearing out as you are sawing.

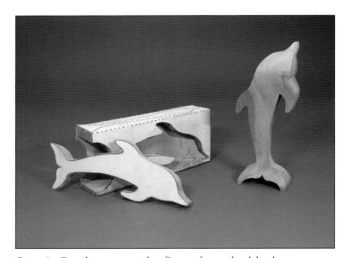

Step 5. Cut the right side, in one continuous line. (If the pattern has legs, cutting between the legs first.)

Step 6. Gently remove the figure from the block.

The "Trapping" Method

I developed this method for cutting tiny figures, such as the accessories for the Wade clock shelves. (See the pattern and photo on page 14.) Because the figure is trapped in the block by the spare stock, it isn't necessary to tape around it after the first cut.

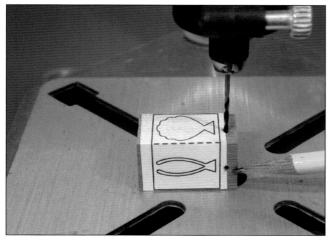

Step 1. Drill starter holes in each side.

Step 2. Thread the blade through the starter hole and cut out the left side.

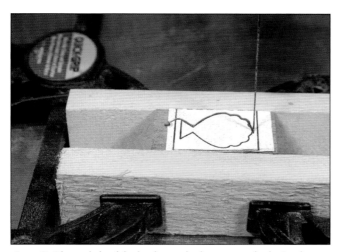

Step 3. Thread the blade through the starter hole in the right side. Make the second cut.

Step 4. Gently remove the figure from the block.

Small figures to sit on shelves of Wade Clock

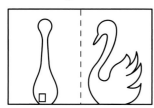 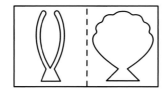 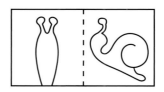

Cut according to "trapping" method

Practice page

The most frustrating part of compound sawing is having a figure come out distorted. In the beginning this caused me so many problems I was ready to throw my saw out the shop door. At one time, I thought "maybe" I can't do this, but I'm just stubborn enough not to give up.

The starting point is to read through the trouble shooting section in the first chapter. Then review the step-by-step instructions. The next step is to practice, practice, practice.

To help beginners, I've developed this practice page. For the best results and less frustration, use with the softest wood available, such as sugar pine, white pine or basswood. Start with the smallest figure and work your way up to cutting the largest one. The #5 blade can be run at 1800 strokes per minute without breaking, but that doesn't mean you can't slow it down until you have a little better control over your saw.

As you progress through the sizes, you will discover a feel for the subtle changes as the wood gets thicker. Of course, by then, you're sick of dolphins and will never cut another one; but they'll all be straight, with no distortions!

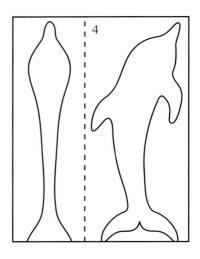

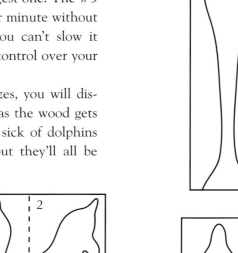

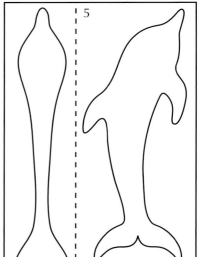

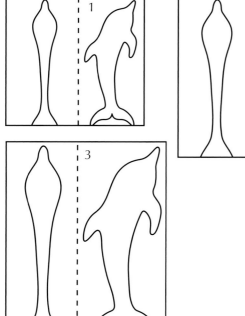

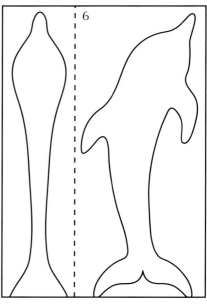

Crackle

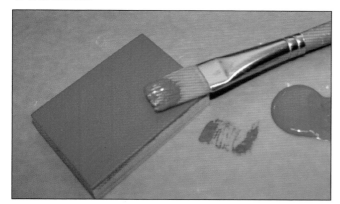

Step 1. Apply several medium thick coats of acrylic craft paint. Choose your favorite brand. Allow it to dry at least four hours.

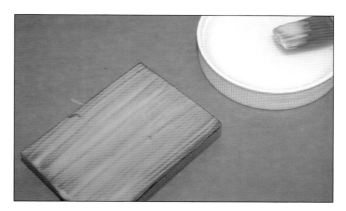

Step 2. Apply a single coat of the crackle medium. The thicker the medium is applied, the bigger the crackles. This is a medium-thick application. The cracks will begin to appear as the medium dries.

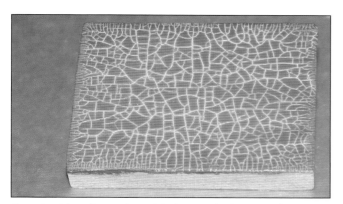

Step 3. After the project dried, I used white acrylic paint to fill in the cracks. Rub it on with your fingers, and wipe excess off with a dry clothe. You may want to thin the paint just a little, but don't over-do it.

This is a sample of how the finished projects can look. It's a very easy finishing technique, but looks impressive. Apply a clear spray finish to protect the surface, and you're done.

Flocking

Flocking gives a smooth, felt-like texture to your projects. Apply the glue in a smooth, generous coat. Immediately apply the fibers. Don't shake or tap the fibers off. Allow your project to dry at least an hour before handling it. Brush off the excess fibers and return them to the bottle.

When using flocking on a compound figure, first apply a water-base sealer to your project. Allow it to dry, then sand it smooth with 220-grit sandpaper. Follow the application directions on the bottle. The details are easily applied over the dry flocking with acrylic craft paints and a small brush.

Sandstone

This is a simple finish called Sandstone by DecoArt. It has a stone-like quality. Simply apply the color of choice, allow it to dry, then apply the next color. It can be top coated with a clear acrylic spray, but it isn't necessary. I prefer leaving it natural, as the texture has a quite pleasing effect.

Apply a water base sealer to your project. Allow it to dry, then sand smooth with 220 or higher grit sandpaper. Apply colors one at a time, using a relatively heavy coat for perfect coverage. Allow it to dry before adding additional colors.

The finished project.

Goldleaf

For this finishing technique, I've used a gold leafing kit, found at most craft stores. It's a very easy, and quick process.

The first step is to apply a sealer to your project, allow it to dry, and sand it smooth with 220 grit sandpaper. Then add a base coat of color, if desired.

Apply one coat of the adhesive. It will be cloudy when first applied. Allow it to dry until it becomes clear.

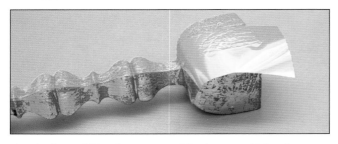

Apply the gold leafing, matte side down, rubbing it firmly with your fingers. Pull the sheet away. The leafing will adhere to your project. Continue this process until your project is covered. A clear coat finish can applied, if desired, upon completion.

I chose to allow the red craft paint of the base coat to show through the gold. The base coat can be covered completely with additional applications of the gold leaf.

Compound Clocks

You will find a few slight differences in the clock directions, due to the different designs. I've chosen to cut the Wade clock in the demonstration to give you a general idea of how the clocks are made. For instance, the weight must be glued into the Wade because a screw would protrude through the bottom shelf. This is also true for the James, the Boyd, the Jackie T, the Captain Bob, and the Papa Clyde. Weights can be screwed or glued into the Jesse, the Aunt Tee, the Colleen and the Marie. These weights are necessary to counter the weight of the clock insert in the top of the piece. The Connie and the Marsha don't require weights.

Note: You will notice several circles in the clock opening on each pattern. This is to give you a choice of inserts.

Inner circle.... ⅞" insert

Middle circle... 1" insert

Outer circle... 1⅛" insert

Special supplies

- Weight bashing jig, pictured at right
- Two pieces of stock, ¾" by 1½" by the length of clock
- 1⅛", 1" or 15/16" micro clock insert
- ⅞" Forstner bit
- ¾ oz. egg sinker (fishing weight)
- 4 X ¾ flathead screws (optional)
- Epoxy glue

Clock Weight Bashing Jig

To make the weight bashing jig, drill a ⅞"-wide hole through a ¼"-thick piece of scrap stock. Sit weight inside jig and bash it down, level to the surface, with a hammer. Note: This jig differs from the jig used to bash weights for the candlesticks in that the wood for the jig is thinner.

Drill a ⅛" hole in the center, and carve out a countersink with a craft knife.

Making the Wade Clock

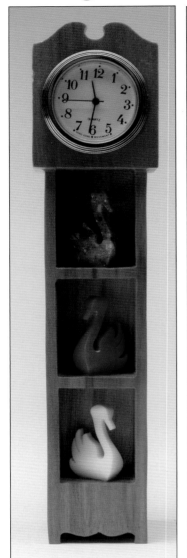

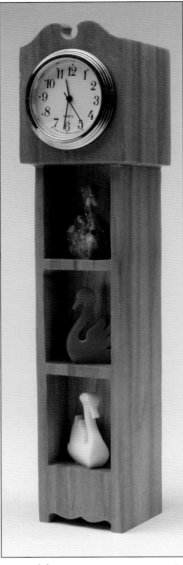

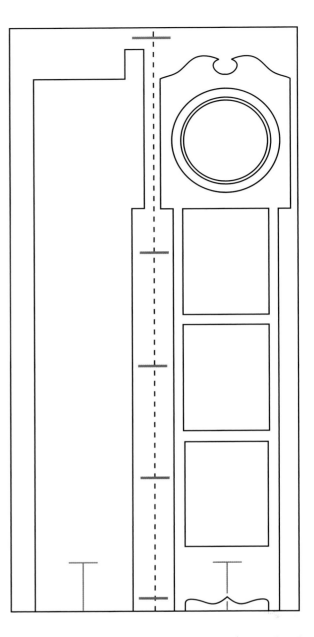

Patterns for the small compound figures appear on page 9.

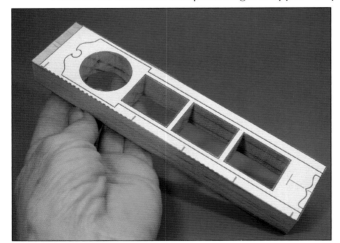

Step 1 Cut the pattern in half, along the dashed line. Adhere the right side to one piece of the stock and cut out the openings.

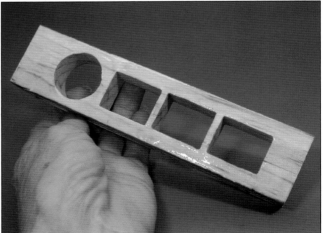

Step 2 Apply wood glue to the underside, being careful to wipe out any glue that may have run down into the openings

Step 3 Clamp the two pieces of stock together and allow the piece to set for at least one hour.

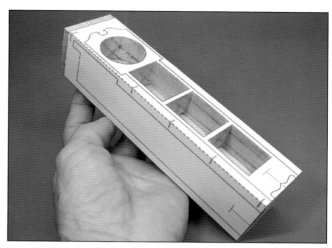

Step 4 Adhere the left side of the pattern to the block, being sure the register marks are lined up perfectly.

Step 5 Mark the bottom as shown to make sure the bottom hole is drilled in the proper place. Measure relative to the center line on each side of the pattern for perfect placement.

Step 6 With a 7/8" Forstner bit, drill the bottom hole to the depth line. A helpful tip: Place your project in a vise for this step.

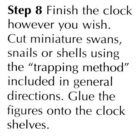

Step 7 Use the weight bashing jig (pictured on page 13) to create the bottom weight. Glue in the weight.

Step 8 Finish the clock however you wish. Cut miniature swans, snails or shells using the "trapping method" included in general directions. Glue the figures onto the clock shelves.

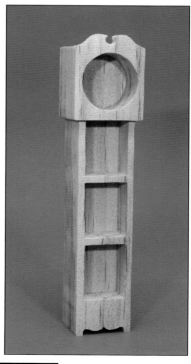

Colleen

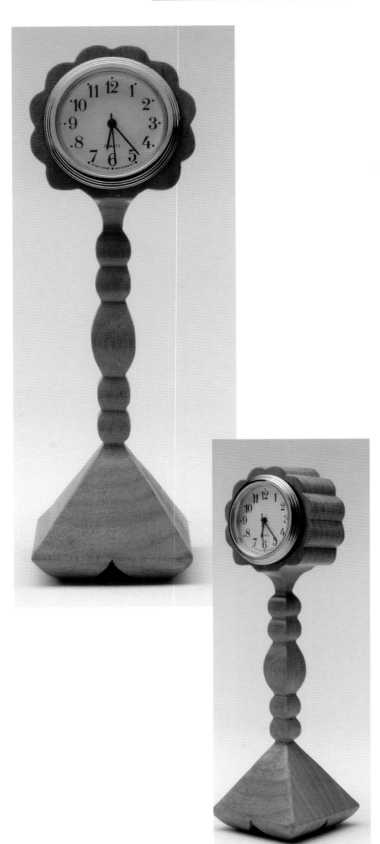

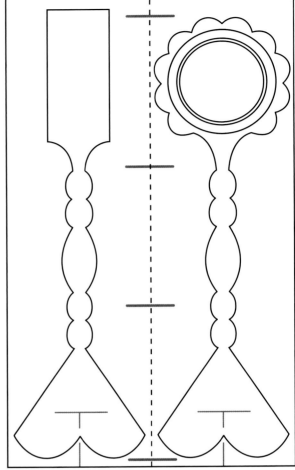

© Diana Thompson

1. Cut the pattern along the dashed line.
2. Adhere the right side of the pattern to one piece of stock.
3. Cut out the insert opening.
4. Glue the two pieces of stock together.
5. Adhere the left side of the pattern to the block, lining up the register marks.
6. With a 7/8" Forstner bit, drill the hole in the bottom to the depth line.
7. With 5/64" drill bit, drill a 3/8" deep screw starter hole in the bottom. (The screw may be omitted and the weight glued in with epoxy glue.)
8. Cut the left side, tape, then cut the right side.
9. Bash down the egg sinker, using the jig.
10. Drill a hole in the center of weight with a 1/8" bit.
11. Carve a countersink in one side of the weight with a craft knife.
12. With a 4 X 3/4 flathead screw, screw the weight into the bottom of the clock.
13. Finish as desired.

Papa Clyde

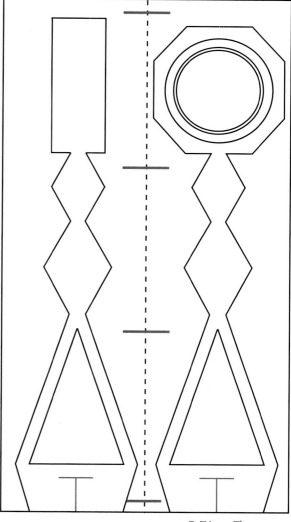

© Diana Thompson

1. Cut the pattern along the dashed line.
2. Adhere the right side of the pattern to one piece of stock.
3. Cut out the insert opening.
4. Glue the two pieces of stock together.
5. Adhere the left side of the pattern to the block, lining up the register marks.
6. With a 7/8" Forstner bit, drill a hole in the bottom to the depth line.
7. Cut the frets from the right side and retain for further use.
8. Cut the frets from left side, if called for, and discard.
9. Continue cutting the left side.
10. Return the frets to the right side, tape, and continue cutting the right side.
11. Bash down the egg sinker with the jig.
12. Glue the weight into the bottom with plenty of epoxy glue.
13. Finish as desired.

Marsha

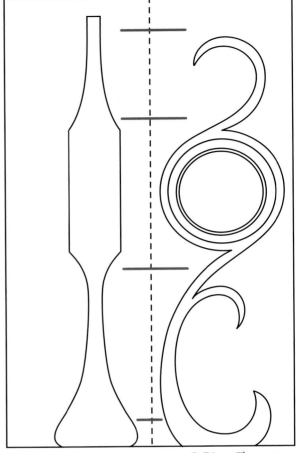

© Diana Thompson

1. Cut the pattern along the dashed line.
2. Adhere the right side of the pattern to one piece of the stock.
3. Cut out the insert opening.
4. Glue the two pieces of stock together.
5. Adhere the left side of the pattern to the block, lining up the register marks.
6. Cut the left side, tape, then cut the right side.
7. Finish as desired.

Marie

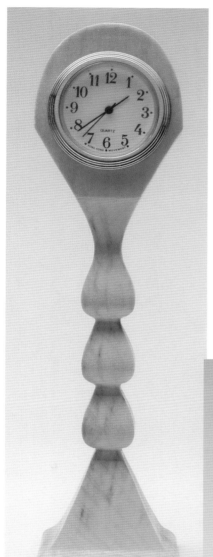

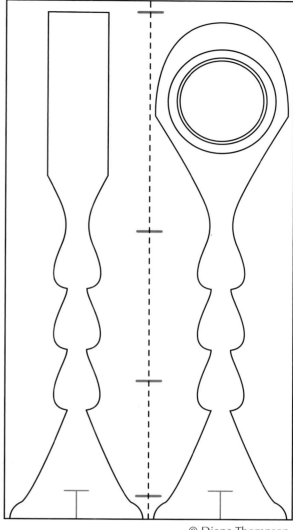

100%

© Diana Thompson

1. Cut the pattern along the dashed line.
2. Adhere the right side of the pattern to one piece of stock.
3. Cut out the insert opening.
4. Glue the two pieces of stock together.
5. Adhere the left side of the pattern to the block, lining up the register marks.
6. With a 7/8" Forstner bit, drill the hole in the bottom to the depth line.
7. With 5/64" drill bit, drill a 3/8" deep screw starter hole in the bottom. (The screw may be omitted and the weight glued in with epoxy glue.)
8. Cut the left side, tape, then cut the right side.
9. Bash down the egg sinker, using the jig.
10. Drill a hole in the center of weight with a 1/8" bit.
11. Carve a countersink in one side of the weight with a craft knife.
12. With a 4 X 3/4 flathead screw, screw the weight into the bottom of the clock.
13. Finish as desired.

James

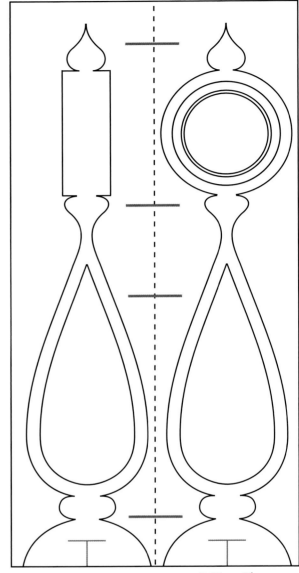

© Diana Thompson

1. Cut the pattern along the dashed line.
2. Adhere the right side of the pattern to one piece of stock.
3. Cut out the insert opening.
4. Glue the two pieces of stock together.
5. Adhere the left side of the pattern to the block, lining up the register marks.
6. With a 7/8" Forstner bit, drill a hole in the bottom to the depth line.
7. Cut the frets from the right side and retain for further use.
8. Cut the frets from left side, if called for, and discard.
9. Continue cutting the left side.
10. Return the frets to the right side, tape, and continue cutting the right side.
11. Bash down the egg sinker with the jig.
12. Glue the weight into the bottom with plenty of epoxy glue.
13. Finish as desired.

Connie

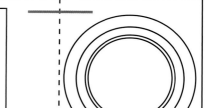

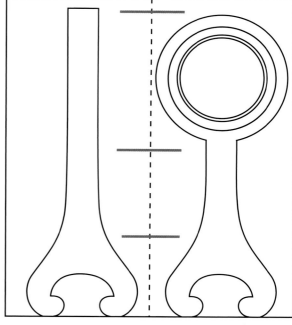

© Diana Thompson

1. Cut the pattern along the dashed line.
2. Adhere the right side of the pattern to one piece of the stock.
3. Cut out the insert opening.
4. Glue the two pieces of stock together.
5. Adhere the left side of the pattern to the block, lining up the register marks.
6. Cut the left side, tape, then cut the right side.
7. Finish as desired.

Aunt Tee

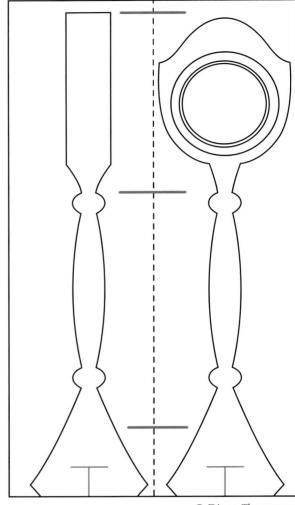

© Diana Thompson

1. Cut the pattern along the dashed line.
2. Adhere the right side of the pattern to one piece of stock.
3. Cut out the insert opening.
4. Glue the two pieces of stock together.
5. Adhere the left side of the pattern to the block, lining up the register marks.
6. With a 7/8" Forstner bit, drill the hole in the bottom to the depth line.
7. With 5/64" drill bit, drill a 3/8" deep screw starter hole in the bottom. (The screw may be omitted and the weight glued in with epoxy glue.)
8. Cut the left side, tape, then cut the right side.
9. Bash down the egg sinker, using the jig.
10. Drill a hole in the center of weight with a 1/8" bit.
11. Carve a countersink in one side of the weight with a craft knife.
12. With a 4 X 3/4 flathead screw, screw the weight into the bottom of the clock.
13. Finish as desired.

Boyd

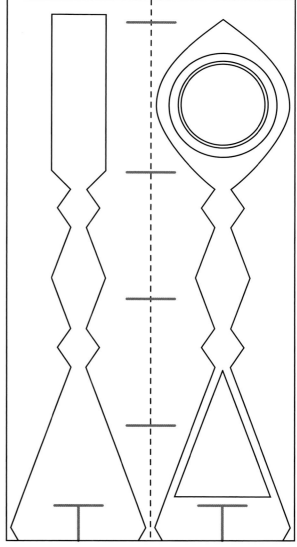

© Diana Thompson

1. Cut the pattern along the dashed line.
2. Adhere the right side of the pattern to one piece of stock.
3. Cut out the insert opening.
4. Glue the two pieces of stock together.
5. Adhere the left side of the pattern to the block, lining up the register marks.
6. With a 7/8" Forstner bit, drill a hole in the bottom to the depth line.
7. Cut the frets from the right side and retain for further use.
8. Cut the frets from left side, if called for, and discard.
9. Continue cutting the left side.
10. Return the frets to the right side, tape, and continue cutting the right side.
11. Bash down the egg sinker with the jig.
12. Glue the weight into the bottom with plenty of epoxy glue.
13. Finish as desired.

Captain Bob

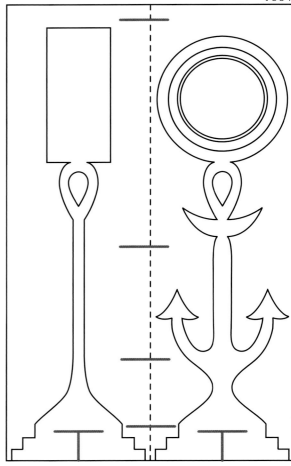

© Diana Thompson

1. Cut the pattern along the dashed line.
2. Adhere the right side of the pattern to one piece of stock.
3. Cut out the insert opening.
4. Glue the two pieces of stock together.
5. Adhere the left side of the pattern to the block, lining up the register marks.
6. With a 7/8" Forstner bit, drill a hole in the bottom to the depth line.
7. Cut the frets from the right side and retain for further use.
8. Cut the frets from left side, if called for, and discard.
9. Continue cutting the left side.
10. Return the frets to the right side, tape, and continue cutting the right side.
11. Bash down the egg sinker with the jig.
12. Glue the weight into the bottom with plenty of epoxy glue.
13. Finish as desired.

Jackie T

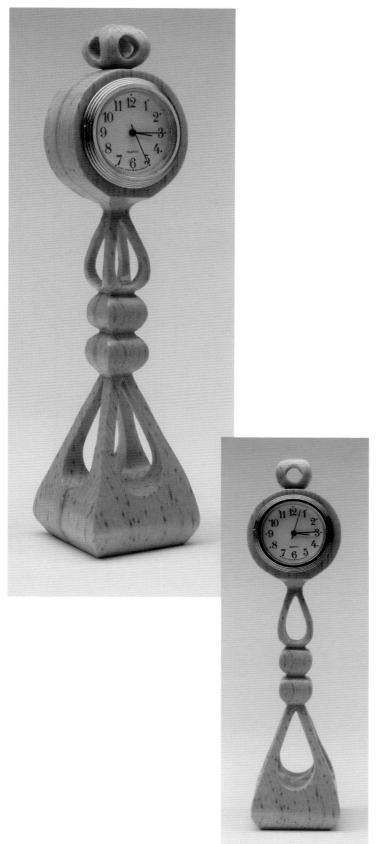

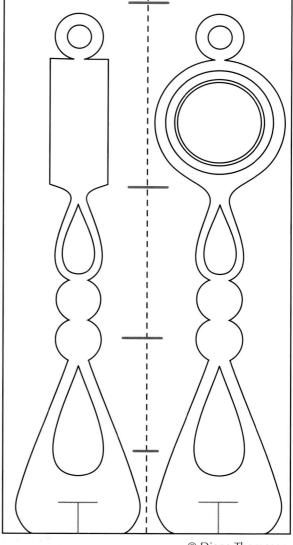

100%

© Diana Thompson

1. Cut the pattern along the dashed line.
2. Adhere the right side of the pattern to one piece of stock.
3. Cut out the insert opening.
4. Glue the two pieces of stock together.
5. Adhere the left side of the pattern to the block, lining up the register marks.
6. With a 7/8" Forstner bit, drill a hole in the bottom to the depth line.
7. Cut the frets from the right side and retain for further use.
8. Cut the frets from left side, if called for, and discard.
9. Continue cutting the left side.
10. Return the frets to the right side, tape, and continue cutting the right side.
11. Bash down the egg sinker with the jig.
12. Glue the weight into the bottom with plenty of epoxy glue.
13. Finish as desired.

Jesse

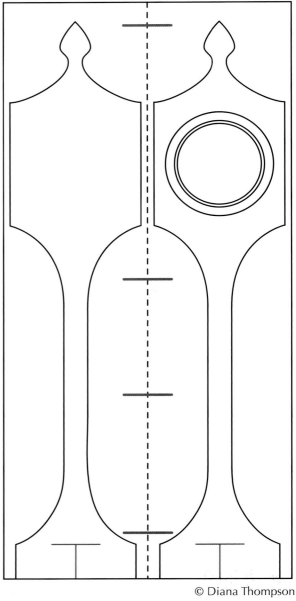

© Diana Thompson

1. Cut the pattern along the dashed line.
2. Adhere the right side of the pattern to one piece of stock.
3. Cut out the insert opening.
4. Glue the two pieces of stock together.
5. Adhere the left side of the pattern to the block, lining up the register marks.
6. With a 7/8" Forstner bit, drill the hole in the bottom to the depth line.
7. With 5/64" drill bit, drill a 3/8" deep screw starter hole in the bottom. (The screw may be omitted and the weight glued in with epoxy glue.)
8. Cut the left side, tape, then cut the right side.
9. Bash down the egg sinker, using the jig.
10. Drill a hole in the center of weight with a 1/8" bit.
11. Carve a countersink in one side of the weight with a craft knife.
12. With a 4 X 3/4 flathead screw, screw the weight into the bottom of the clock.
13. Finish as desired.

CHAPTER FIVE

Compound Candlesticks

Last year, I was given a drill press as a Christmas present. Not long after that I discovered a Forstner bit in the bottom of my husband's tool box. That led to my fascination with Forstner bits. I drilled holes in everything. As it happens, I keep a bee's wax candle near my saw for lubricating my saw blades. One day, I stuck the candle in the hole of one of the many scrapes I had "Forstnerized" just to keep it handy beside the saw. That lead to the candlestick designs.

I almost scraped the idea after they kept falling over once a candle was placed in them. They needed a counterweight. Being an angler all my life, the first thing I thought to use was a lead fishing weight. The nicest thing about them is they're readily available and easy to bash into shape!

Special Supplies

You will need stock: $1^1/2$" x $1^1/2$" x the length of candle stick. You may also glue together two pieces of stock measuring $3/4$" x $1^1/2$" x the length of candle stick.

$7/8$" Forstner bit
1 oz. egg sinker
4 x $3/4$ flathead screws
Epoxy glue
Weight bashing jig

Candlestick Weight Bashing Jig

To make jig, drill a $7/8$"-wide hole through a $3/8$"-thick piece of scrap stock. Sit weight inside jig and bash it down, level to the surface, with a hammer. Note: This jig differs from the clock weight bashing jib in that the wood is thicker.

Drill a $1/8$" hole in the center, and carve out a countersink with a craft knife.

Making the "Charming" Candlestick

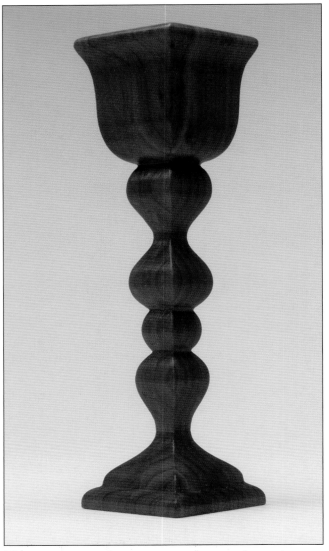

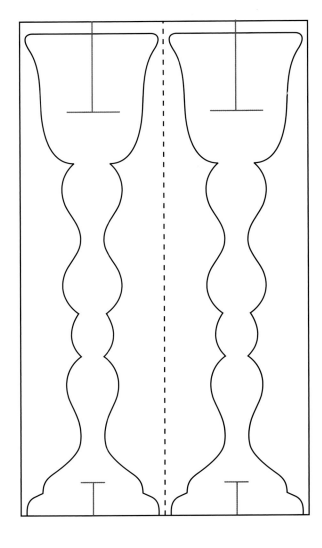

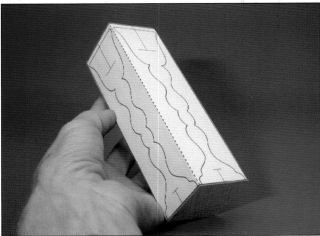

Step 1 Adhere the pattern to the stock with spray adhesive.

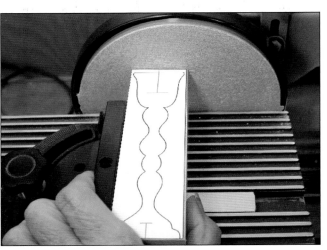

Step 2 Make sure that each end of the pattern is square.

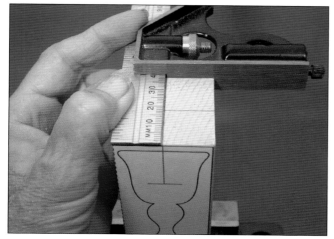

Step 3 Mark the bottom as shown to make sure the bottom hole is drilled in the proper place. Measure relative to the center line on each side of the pattern for perfect placement.

Step 4 With a 7/8" Forstner bit, drill the top hole to the depth line. A helpful tip: Place your project in a vise for this step. Repeat this step for the bottom hole.

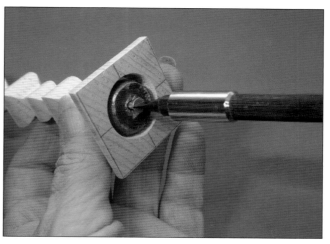

Step 5 With a 5/64" bit, drill a starter hole in the bottom. From this point, cut the candlestick as any other compound pattern.

Step 6 Screw the weight into the bottom or use epoxy to glue it in.

Step 7 Your project is complete and ready to finish as desired.

Classic

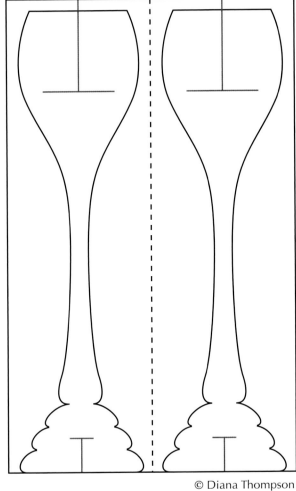

100%

© Diana Thompson

1 Apply the pattern to the wood according to the general directions.
2 Cut or sand the bottom and the top of the stock even with the pattern rectangle.
3 Clamp the project in a vise.
4 Mark the center, using the depth line (in center of each side of the pattern) on each side.
5 Drill the hole with a 7/8" Forstner bit to the depth line.
6 Repeat the process on the other end of the figure.
7 With a 5/64" drill bit, drill a 3/8" deep screw starter hole in the bottom hole.
8 Cut out the frets, where called for, on each side.
9 Cut the left side, tape, cut the right side.
10 Bash down the egg sinker using the jig.
11 Drill a hole in the center of the weight with a 1/8" bit.
12 Carve a counter sick in one side of the weight with a craft knife.
13 With a 4 X 3/4 flathead screw, screw the weight into the bottom of the candlestick.
14 Finish as desired.

Cheerful Tulip

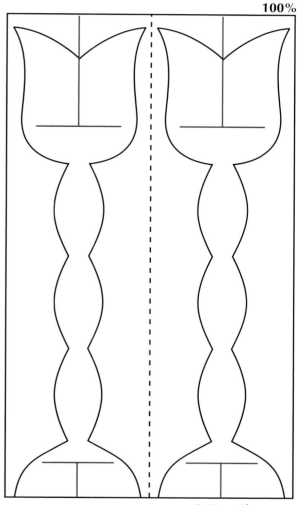

© Diana Thompson

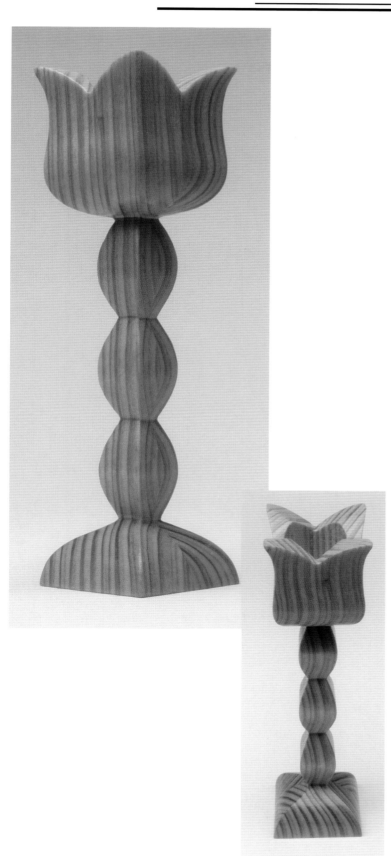

1 Apply the pattern to the wood according to the general directions.
2 Cut or sand the bottom and the top of the stock even with the pattern rectangle.
3 Clamp the project in a vise.
4 Mark the center, using the depth line (in center of each side of the pattern) on each side.
5 Drill the hole with a 7/8" Forstner bit to the depth line.
6 Repeat the process on the other end of the figure.
7 With a 5/64" drill bit, drill a 3/8" deep screw starter hole in the bottom hole.
8 Cut out the frets, where called for, on each side.
9 Cut the left side, tape, cut the right side.
10 Bash down the egg sinker using the jig.
11 Drill a hole in the center of the weight with a 1/8" bit.
12 Carve a counter sick in one side of the weight with a craft knife.
13 With a 4 X 3/4 flathead screw, screw the weight into the bottom of the candlestick.
14 Finish as desired.

Whimsical Lace

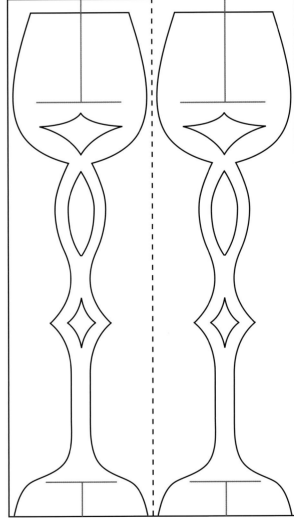

© Diana Thompson

1 Apply the pattern to the wood according to the general directions.
2 Cut or sand the bottom and the top of the stock even with the pattern rectangle.
3 Clamp the project in a vise.
4 Mark the center, using the depth line (in center of each side of the pattern) on each side.
5 Drill the hole with a 7/8" Forstner bit to the depth line.
6 Repeat the process on the other end of the figure.
7 With a 5/64" drill bit, drill a 3/8" deep screw starter hole in the bottom hole.
8 Cut out the frets, where called for, on each side.
9 Cut the left side, tape, cut the right side.
10 Bash down the egg sinker using the jig.
11 Drill a hole in the center of the weight with a 1/8" bit.
12 Carve a counter sick in one side of the weight with a craft knife.
13 With a 4 X 3/4 flathead screw, screw the weight into the bottom of the candlestick.
14 Finish as desired.

Regal Royalty

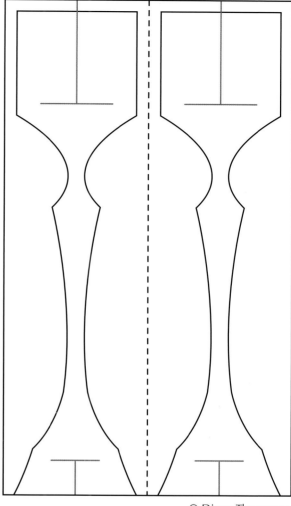

© Diana Thompson

1 Apply the pattern to the wood according to the general directions.
2 Cut or sand the bottom and the top of the stock even with the pattern rectangle.
3 Clamp the project in a vise.
4 Mark the center, using the depth line (in center of each side of the pattern) on each side.
5 Drill the hole with a 7/8" Forstner bit to the depth line.
6 Repeat the process on the other end of the figure.
7 With a 5/64" drill bit, drill a 3/8" deep screw starter hole in the bottom hole.
8 Cut out the frets, where called for, on each side.
9 Cut the left side, tape, cut the right side.
10 Bash down the egg sinker using the jig.
11 Drill a hole in the center of the weight with a 1/8" bit.
12 Carve a counter sick in one side of the weight with a craft knife.
13 With a 4 X 3/4 flathead screw, screw the weight into the bottom of the candlestick.
14 Finish as desired.

Graceful Lady

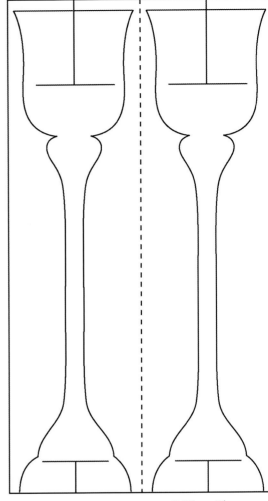

100%

© Diana Thompson

1 Apply the pattern to the wood according to the general directions.
2 Cut or sand the bottom and the top of the stock even with the pattern rectangle.
3 Clamp the project in a vise.
4 Mark the center, using the depth line (in center of each side of the pattern) on each side.
5 Drill the hole with a 7/8" Forstner bit to the depth line.
6 Repeat the process on the other end of the figure.
7 With a 5/64" drill bit, drill a 3/8" deep screw starter hole in the bottom hole.
8 Cut out the frets, where called for, on each side.
9 Cut the left side, tape, cut the right side.
10 Bash down the egg sinker using the jig.
11 Drill a hole in the center of the weight with a 1/8" bit.
12 Carve a counter sick in one side of the weight with a craft knife.
13 With a 4 X 3/4 flathead screw, screw the weight into the bottom of the candlestick.
14 Finish as desired.

34

Diamond

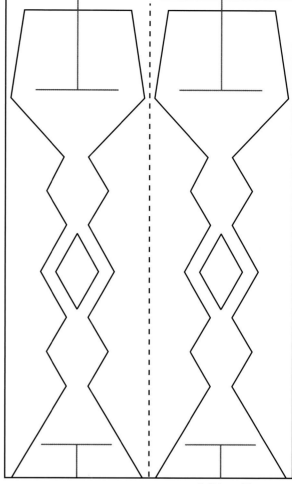

© Diana Thompson

1. Apply the pattern to the wood according to the general directions.
2. Cut or sand the bottom and the top of the stock even with the pattern rectangle.
3. Clamp the project in a vise.
4. Mark the center, using the depth line (in center of each side of the pattern) on each side.
5. Drill the hole with a 7/8" Forstner bit to the depth line.
6. Repeat the process on the other end of the figure.
7. With a 5/64" drill bit, drill a 3/8" deep screw starter hole in the bottom hole.
8. Cut out the frets, where called for, on each side.
9. Cut the left side, tape, cut the right side.
10. Bash down the egg sinker using the jig.
11. Drill a hole in the center of the weight with a 1/8" bit.
12. Carve a counter sick in one side of the weight with a craft knife.
13. With a 4 X 3/4 flathead screw, screw the weight into the bottom of the candlestick.
14. Finish as desired.

Dynasty

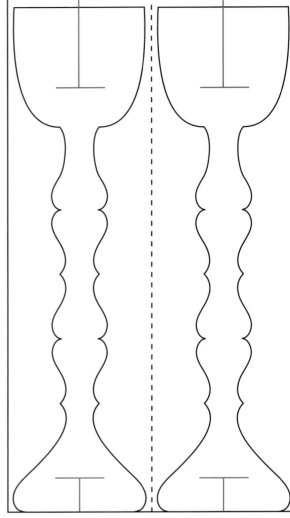

© Diana Thompson

1 Apply the pattern to the wood according to the general directions.
2 Cut or sand the bottom and the top of the stock even with the pattern rectangle.
3 Clamp the project in a vise.
4 Mark the center, using the depth line (in center of each side of the pattern) on each side.
5 Drill the hole with a 7/8" Forstner bit to the depth line.
6 Repeat the process on the other end of the figure.
7 With a 5/64" drill bit, drill a 3/8" deep screw starter hole in the bottom hole.
8 Cut out the frets, where called for, on each side.
9 Cut the left side, tape, cut the right side.
10 Bash down the egg sinker using the jig.
11 Drill a hole in the center of the weight with a 1/8" bit.
12 Carve a counter sick in one side of the weight with a craft knife.
13 With a 4 X 3/4 flathead screw, screw the weight into the bottom of the candlestick.
14 Finish as desired.

Princess

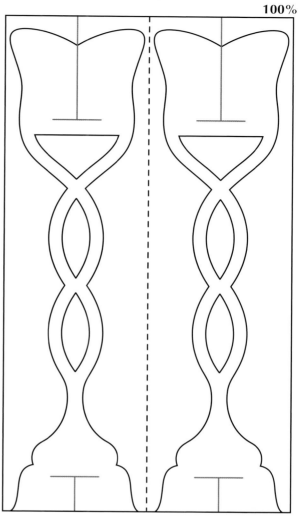

© Diana Thompson

1 Apply the pattern to the wood according to the general directions.
2 Cut or sand the bottom and the top of the stock even with the pattern rectangle.
3 Clamp the project in a vise.
4 Mark the center, using the depth line (in center of each side of the pattern) on each side.
5 Drill the hole with a 7/8" Forstner bit to the depth line.
6 Repeat the process on the other end of the figure.
7 With a 5/64" drill bit, drill a 3/8" deep screw starter hole in the bottom hole.
8 Cut out the frets, where called for, on each side.
9 Cut the left side, tape, cut the right side.
10 Bash down the egg sinker using the jig.
11 Drill a hole in the center of the weight with a 1/8" bit.
12 Carve a counter sick in one side of the weight with a craft knife.
13 With a 4 X 3/4 flathead screw, screw the weight into the bottom of the candlestick.
14 Finish as desired.

Teardrop

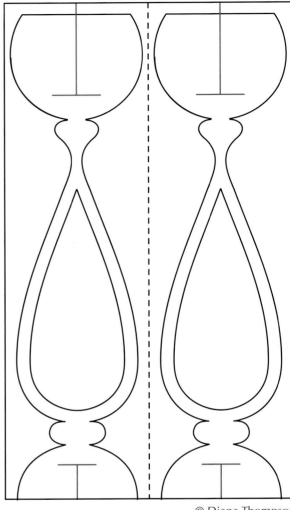

100%

© Diana Thompson

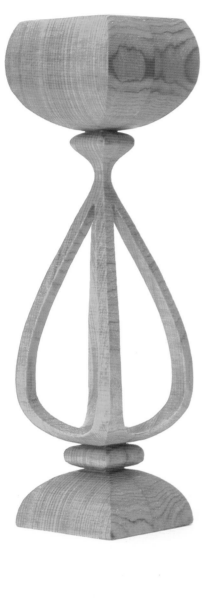

1 Apply the pattern to the wood according to the general directions.
2 Cut or sand the bottom and the top of the stock even with the pattern rectangle.
3 Clamp the project in a vise.
4 Mark the center, using the depth line (in center of each side of the pattern) on each side.
5 Drill the hole with a 7/8" Forstner bit to the depth line.
6 Repeat the process on the other end of the figure.
7 Cut out the fret from the right side and reserve for future use.
8 Cut out the fret from left side and discard.
9 Continue cutting left side.
10 Return the fret to the right side.
11 Tape and cut right side.
12 Bash down the egg sinker using the jig.
13 Glue the weight into the bottom using epoxy glue.
14. Finish as desired.

CHAPTER SIX

Compound Creatures

In this section you will find the results of my whimsical imagination. They're always fun to do because there are no restrictions on how they should look. The sillier they come out, the better!

The two part patterns are due to the encouragement of the legendary designer, John Nelson. My nickname for him has become "the great instigator!"

His imagination is so much more vivid than my own!

The American Eagle pattern is in honor of our wonderful country, dedicated to all who love her, all those in service to defend her, and all those we've lost in defense of her. My goal was to design him as proud as we, the people of the United States of America, are of him.

Hummingbird

100%

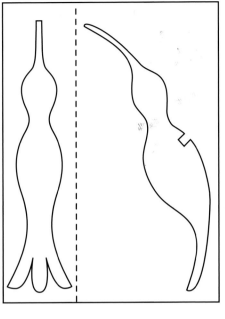

Body

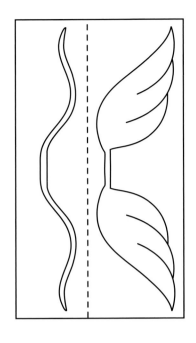

Wings

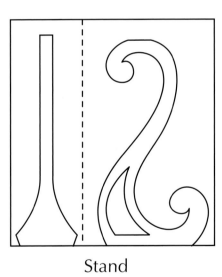

Stand

Cut out all pieces. Glue the wings into the notch on the body. Glue hummingbird to the top of the stand.

Duh!

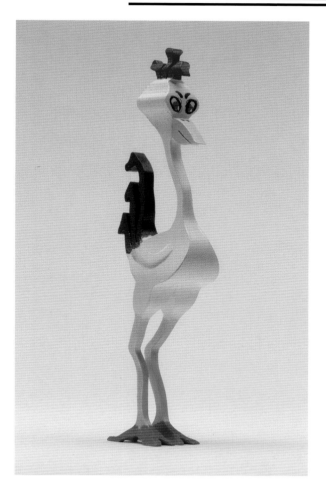

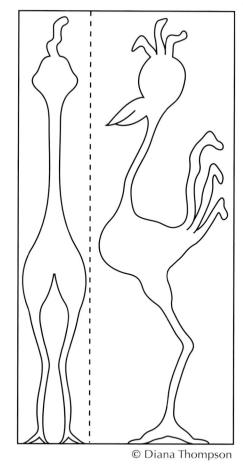

© Diana Thompson

Fats Frog

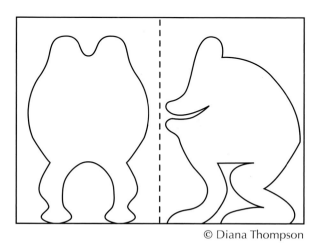

© Diana Thompson

American Eagle

American Eagle

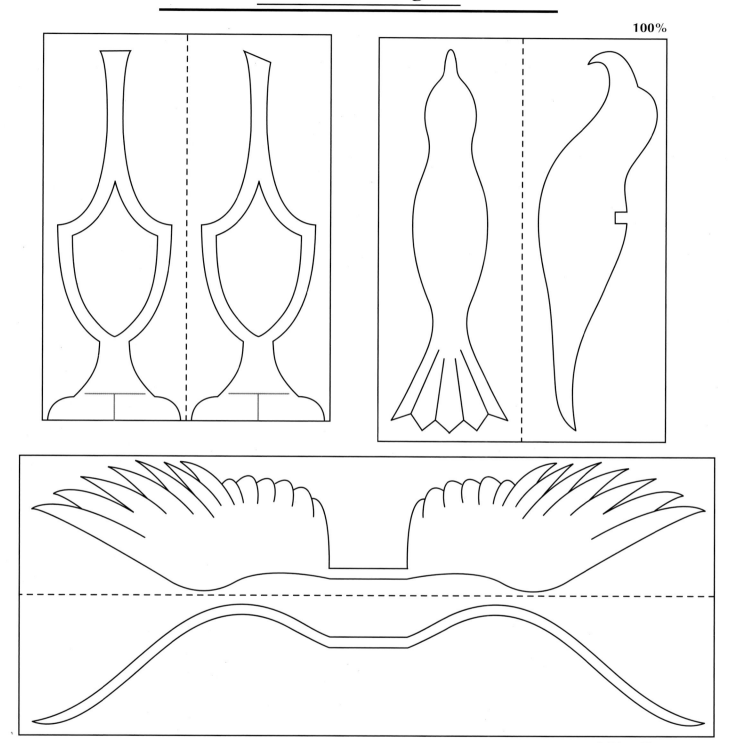

© Diana Thompson

Cut the body and wings according to general directions (cut left side, tape, cut right side)
Glue wings into notch on the body.

With a 5/8" forstner bit, drill a hole in the bottom of the stand to the depth line.
Make a jig (see photos for making jig in the clock and candle stick directions) 1/4" deep, with 5/8"
forstener bit. Bash down a 1/2 oz. egg sinker and glue into bottom of stand.

Butterfly

Large Butterfly

100%

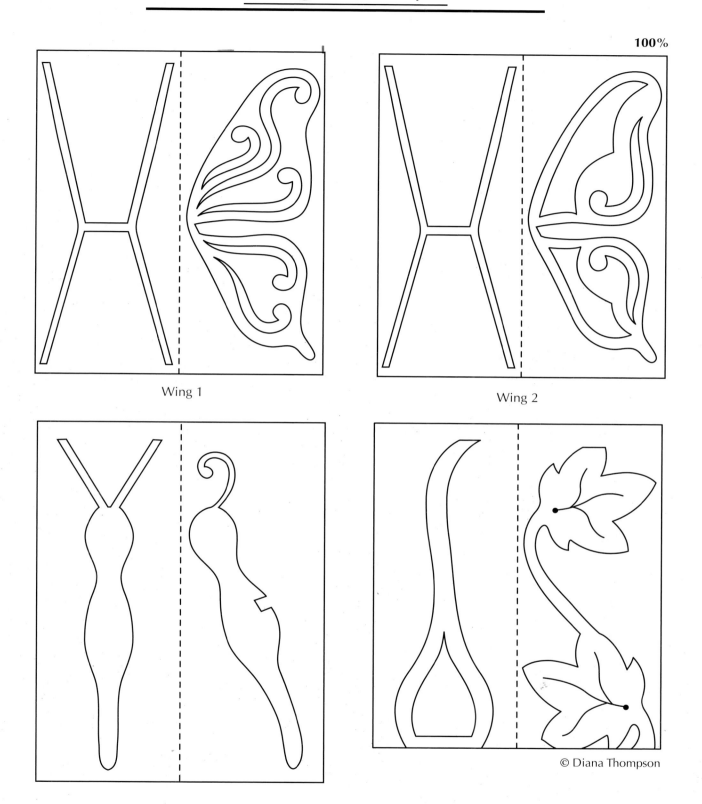

Wing 1

Wing 2

© Diana Thompson

Cut out all pieces. Glue the wings into the notch on the body.

Cowasocky and Friends

Cowasocky and Friends

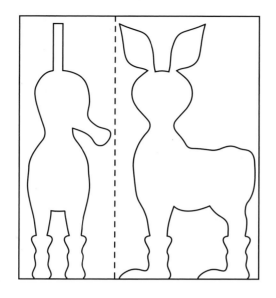

"Cowasocky"

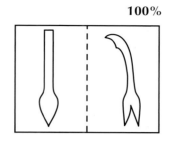

100%

Cut tails according to trapping method in general directions.

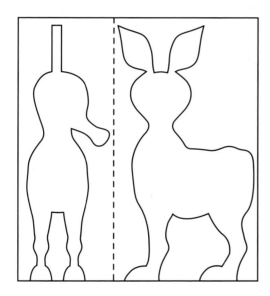

Friend 1

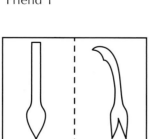

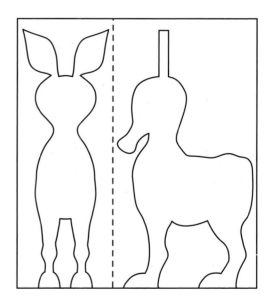

Friend 2

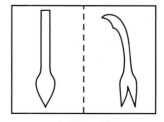

© Diana Thompson

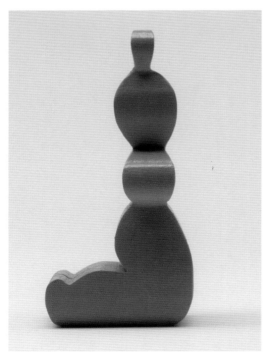

Bear

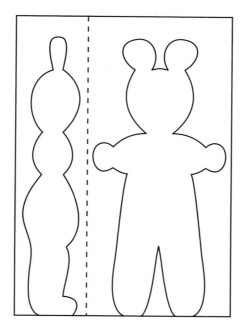

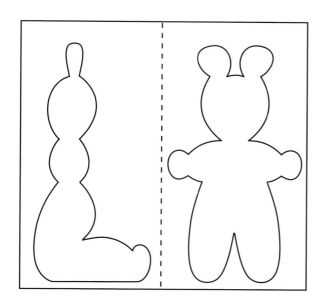

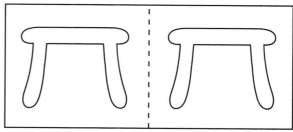

© Diana Thompson

Dolphins

100%

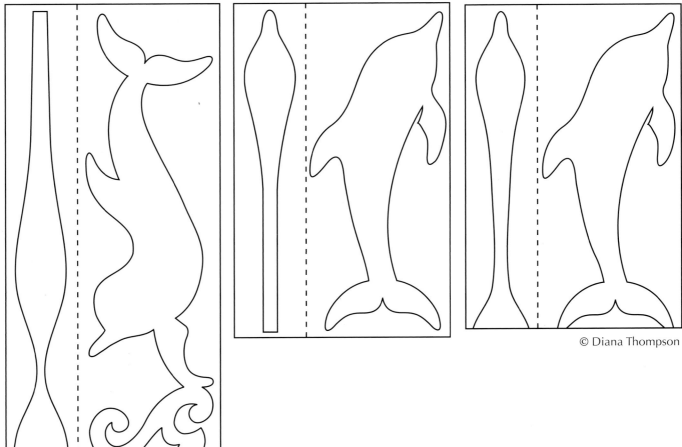

© Diana Thompson

Flamingo

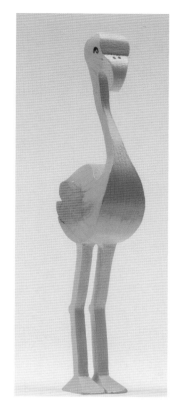

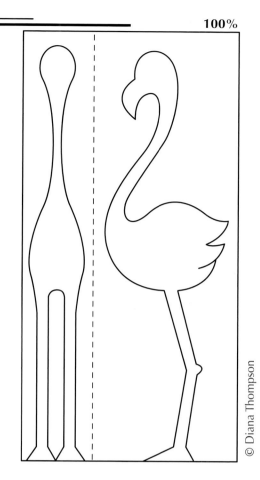

100%

Miss Martha

100%

Compound Scroll Saw Creations

Dragon

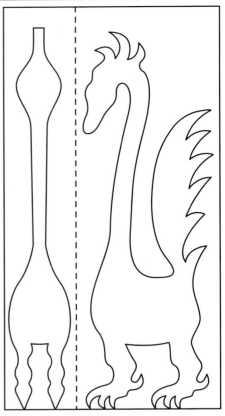

100%

Horse

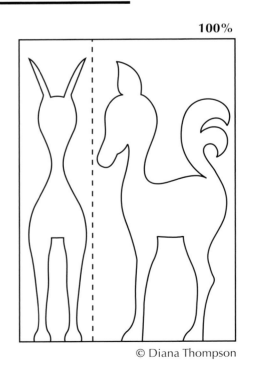

100%

Barb's Caterpillar

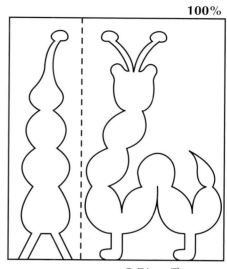

© Diana Thompson

Buzz Bee

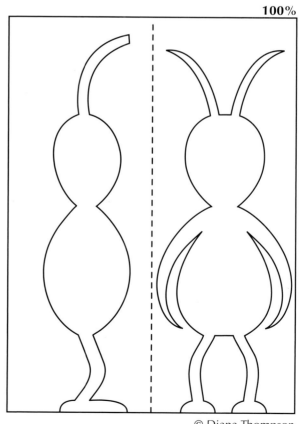

© Diana Thompson

Heron

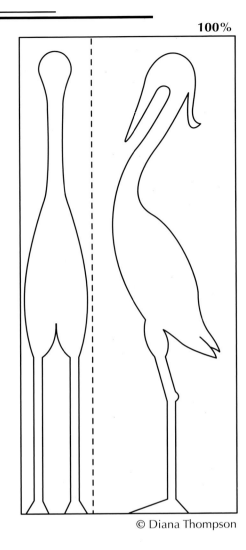

100%

© Diana Thompson

Snail

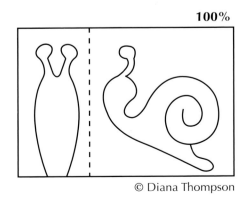

100%

© Diana Thompson

On the House

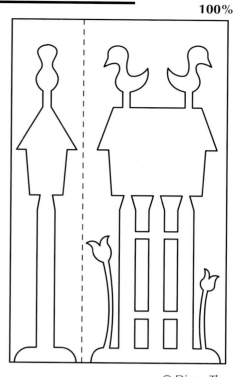

100%

© Diana Thompson

Apple for the Teacher

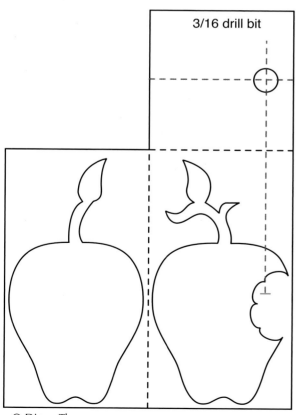

3/16 drill bit

Fold this section over top of stock.

Drill hole to debth line before cuttting pattern.

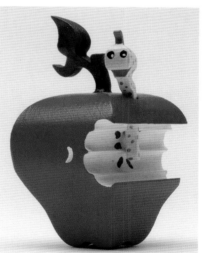

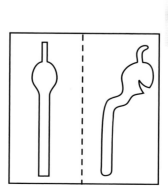

© Diana Thompson

Turtle

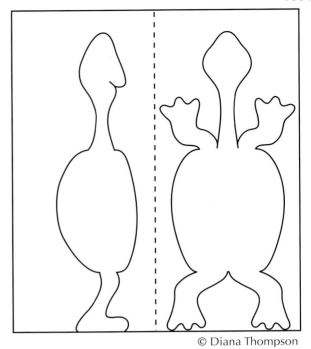

© Diana Thompson

Dragonfly

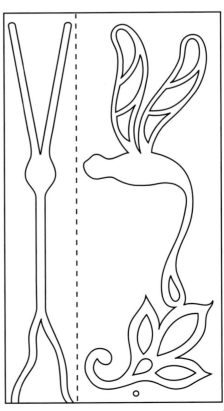

© Diana Thompson

Compound Scroll Saw Creations

Cactus

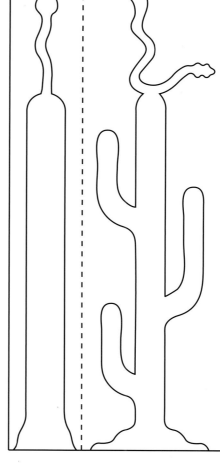

100%

Balancing Act (snake)

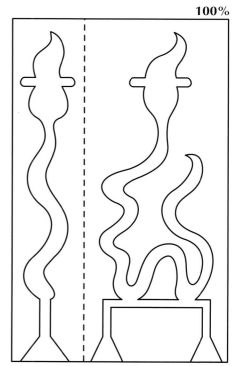

100%

Compound Scroll Saw Creations

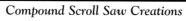

Carousel

Construction notes

The revolving turntable music mechanism that I used in this carousel is available from CherryTree (1–800–848–4363, www.cherrytree-online.com).

You will find all the directions printed on the pattern. I've found this most helpful when making the carousel.

I did the final finish on each piece as it is completed, and before the final assembly. It's much easier and makes for better results.

I used a water-base wood sealer on all of the pieces. After drying, I sanded them smooth with 220-grit sandpaper. Then I applied several coats of clear acrylic spray. I suggest that you apply as many coats as you like to achieve your favorite results.

If you find the pitched roof too difficult, try scrolling a flat roof. The carousel will look just as beautiful.

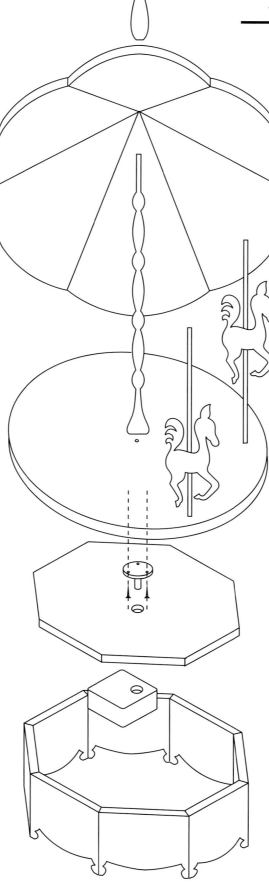

Only two horses
shown for clarity.

Patterns

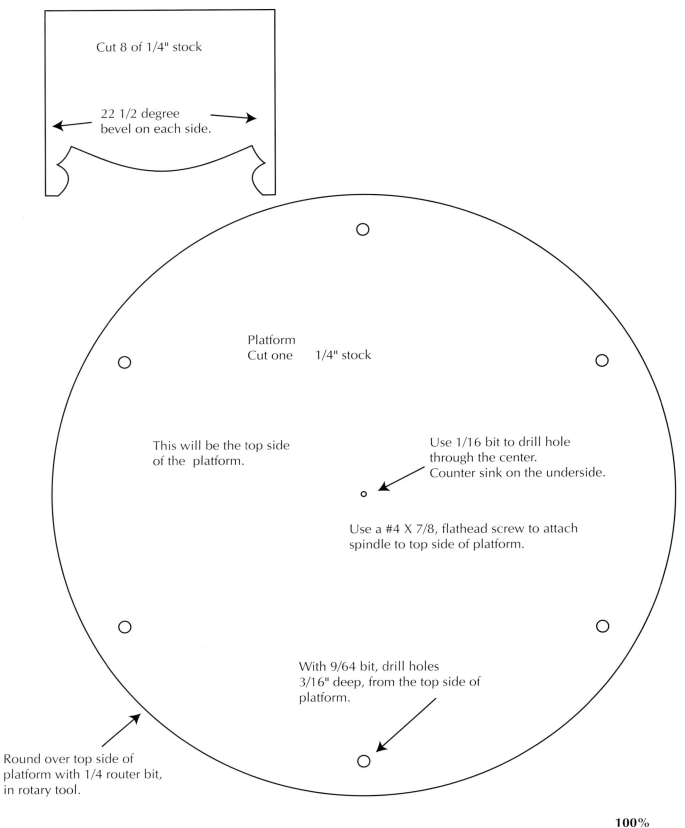

Cut 8 of 1/4" stock

22 1/2 degree
bevel on each side.

Platform
Cut one   1/4" stock

This will be the top side
of the platform.

Use 1/16 bit to drill hole
through the center.
Counter sink on the underside.

Use a #4 X 7/8, flathead screw to attach
spindle to top side of platform.

With 9/64 bit, drill holes
3/16" deep, from the top side of
platform.

Round over top side of
platform with 1/4 router bit,
in rotary tool.

100%

© Diana Thompson

Patterns

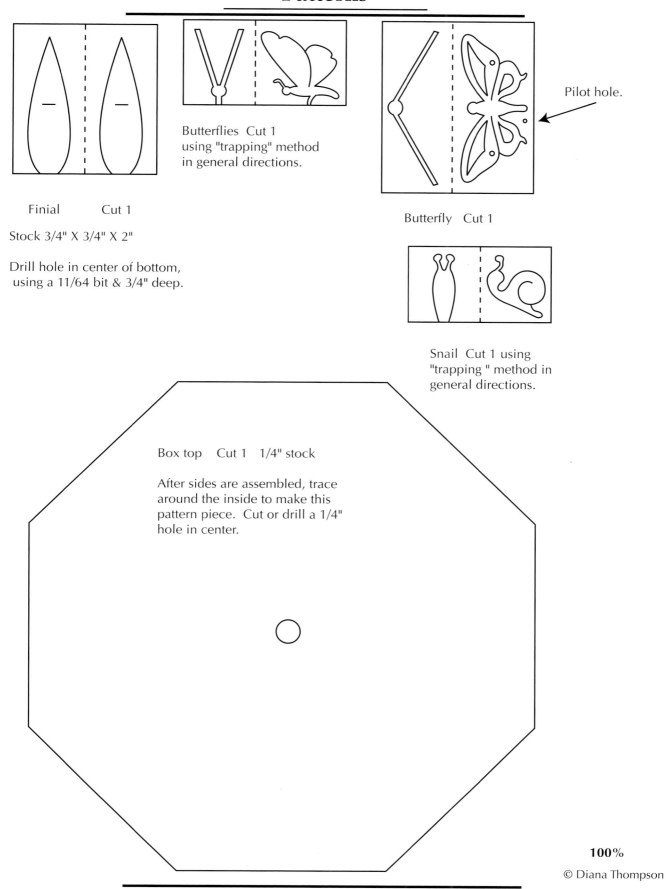

Finial   Cut 1

Stock 3/4" X 3/4" X 2"

Drill hole in center of bottom,
using a 11/64 bit & 3/4" deep.

Butterflies Cut 1
using "trapping" method
in general directions.

Pilot hole.

Butterfly   Cut 1

Snail   Cut 1 using
"trapping " method in
general directions.

Box top   Cut 1   1/4" stock

After sides are assembled, trace
around the inside to make this
pattern piece. Cut or drill a 1/4"
hole in center.

100%

© Diana Thompson

Patterns

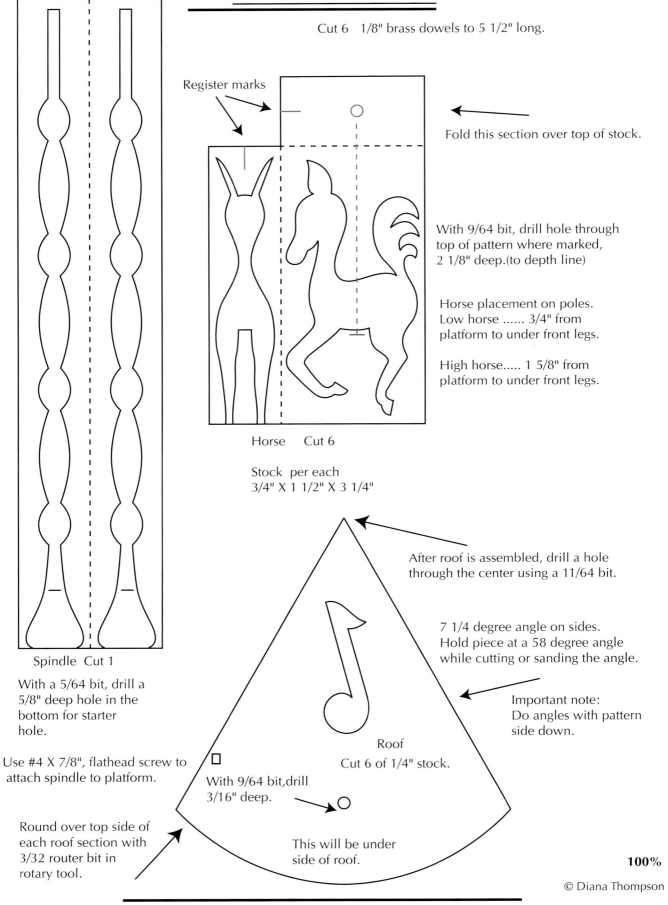

Cut 6   1/8" brass dowels to 5 1/2" long.

Register marks

Fold this section over top of stock.

With 9/64 bit, drill hole through
top of pattern where marked,
2 1/8" deep.(to depth line)

Horse placement on poles.
Low horse ...... 3/4" from
platform to under front legs.

High horse..... 1 5/8" from
platform to under front legs.

Horse   Cut 6

Stock per each
3/4" X 1 1/2" X 3 1/4"

Spindle Cut 1

With a 5/64 bit, drill a
5/8" deep hole in the
bottom for starter
hole.

Use #4 X 7/8", flathead screw to
attach spindle to platform.

Round over top side of
each roof section with
3/32 router bit in
rotary tool.

After roof is assembled, drill a hole
through the center using a 11/64 bit.

7 1/4 degree angle on sides.
Hold piece at a 58 degree angle
while cutting or sanding the angle.

Important note:
Do angles with pattern
side down.

Roof
Cut 6 of 1/4" stock.

With 9/64 bit, drill
3/16" deep.

This will be under
side of roof.

100%

© Diana Thompson

Making the Base

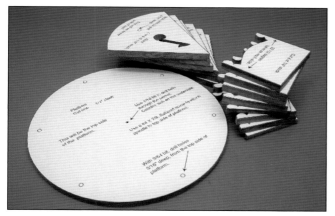

1 Cut out all the pieces.

2 Sand or cut the angles of the side pieces. I prefer to use the disk sander.

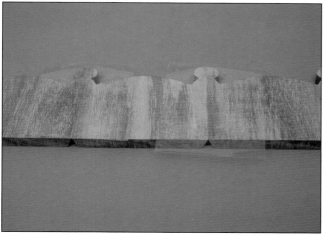

3 Lay the pieces face up in a row. Tape them together with masking tape or packing tape.

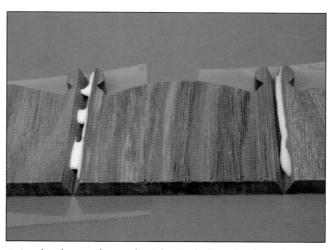

4 Apply glue to the underside, including the last piece.

5 Pull the pieces into a circle and tape the last pieces together. Place three rubber bands around the assembly and allow it to dry.

6 Turn the sides of the assembly upside down and trace around the inside to make the top pattern.

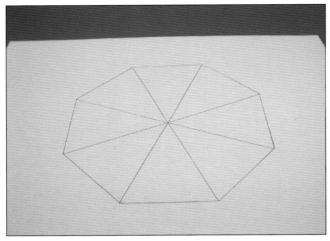

7 The top pattern is ready to cut.

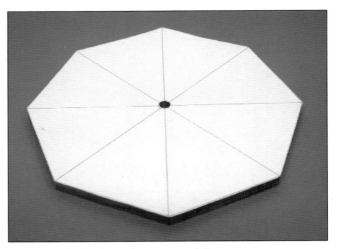

8 Drill a 1/4" hole in the center of the top.

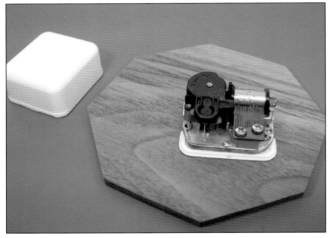

9 Attach a music mechanism to the under side of the top, with a shaft visible through the 1/4" hole. Mechanisms will vary. I attach mine with #2 X 1/2 round head screws. Once attached, replace the cover.

10 With wood glue, glue the top into the side assembly, making sure it is flush to the top. Apply the final finish to this section.

Making the Platform

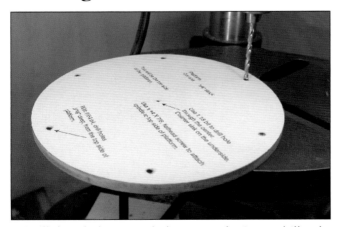

1 Drill dowel placement holes, remembering to drill only 3/16" deep and not all the way through the platform.

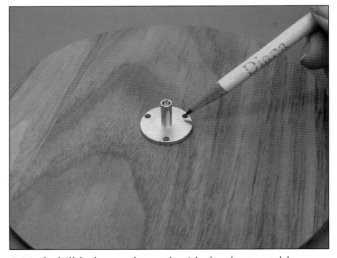

2 Mark drill holes on the underside for the turntable.

3 Drill a small hole in the center of the platform all the way through the piece. At the same time, predrill the turntable screw holes 3/16" deep. Countersink the center hole from the underside of platform.

Making the Roof

1 Drill the dowel placement holes, remembering to only drill 3/16" deep, and not all the way though.

3 Important note: Turn the section over, with the pattern side down, to complete this next step. Otherwise, the roof sections will not meet properly. While holding the piece at a 58 degree angle, top side up, sand a 7 1/4 degree angle on each side edge. To do this step, make a jig with a 45 degree angle as shown in the photo. For the right side of the piece, set your miter guide 13 degrees to the left of 90 degrees.

4 Round over the top side of the platform with a rotary tool and a 3/32" router bit or by hand with sandpaper. Apply the final finish to this section.

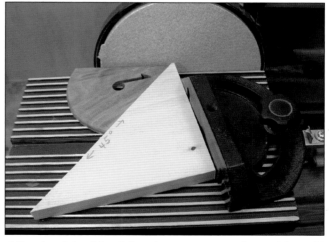

2 Round over the top side of each section with a rotary tool and a 3/32" router bit or by hand with sandpaper.

4 For the right side of the piece, set your miter guide to 13 degrees to the right of 90 degrees.

5 With the top sides up, arrange the six sections in a circle and tape them in place with packing or masking tape.

6 Apply glue to each section on the underside, including the final open section and tape them into place.

7 Once the piece is dry, drill the hole in the center of the roof. Apply the final finish to this section.

Making the Horses

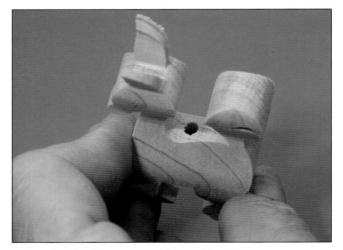

1 Cut six pieces of stock of your choice. (I used a different wood for each horse.) Adhere the pattern to the stock, making sure the register marks line up.

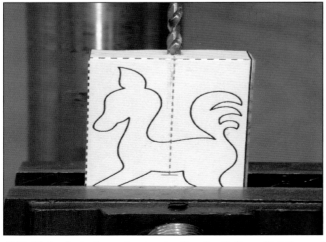

2 Drill the hole from the top to the depth line. Cut the pattern according to the general directions.

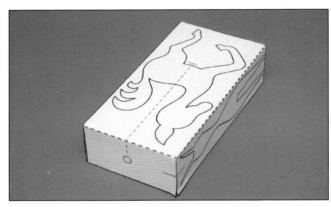

3 Your finished horse should look like this.

4 A bottom view of the finished horse.

Making the Spindle and Finial

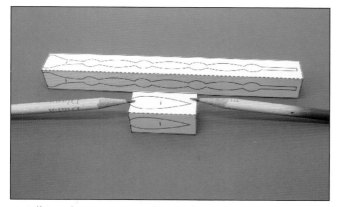

1 Adhere the patterns to the stock, making sure both ends are square.

Making the Brass Dowels

1 Cut six brass dowels, 5 1/2" long. I used a #5 metal cutting blade to cut them on the scroll saw. To make sure they are all the same length, tape them to a scrape of wood and sand them even with a disk sander. Note: Be sure to wear eye protection as the metal dust will fly quite a distance.

5 Apply the final finish to each horse. Helpful hint: Insert open paper clips into the bottoms for handles while spray finishing; then stick the horses into a Styrofoam block to dry.

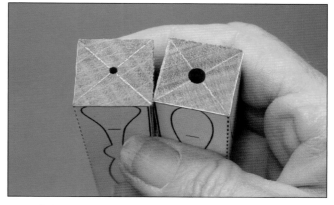

2 Drill the holes in the bottom of each. Make starter holes for the spindles and the insert holes for the finial. Cut according to general directions.

Final Assembly

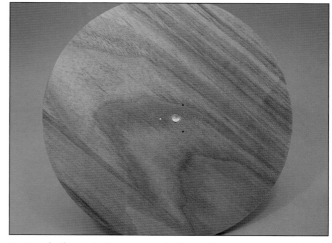

1 Attach the spindle to the platform from the underside.

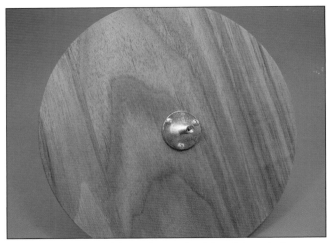

2 Attach the turntable to the underside of the platform.

3 Apply a small amount of epoxy glue inside the dowel holes and insert the dowel. Slide a retaining block over the dowel and clamp it into place. This ensures that the dowel is kept in a vertical position. This can be done all at once or one dowel at a time.

4 Apply epoxy glue to the insides of the holes in the horses and slide them over the dowels. Place the spare blocks, cut to height, under the horse's front legs to hold them in position, alternating high and low. Allow the glue to dry. Helpful tips: Use a toothpick to get glue into holes. Also place a toothpick between the dowel and back of horse head if it wants to lean backwards.

5 Apply a small amount of epoxy glue inside the dowel holes. Slide the roof over the spindle and position the dowels snugly in holes.

To finish the carousel: Apply glue inside the finial and slide it snugly down over spindle. Apply a small amount of glue around spindle where it goes through the underside of the roof. Cut and glue the butterflies and snails in place according to photo or as desired. Screw the turntable shaft into the music box. Turn to wind.

6 Place a small clamp on the spindle top to hold the roof snugly in place until the glue dries.